Instagram Marketing

Grow Your Business Fast with the Help of Instagram and Social Media

Daniel Parker

Table of Contents

Introduction

Thank you for choosing this book on the topic of Instagram marketing! Within the following pages, we will begin to dive into Instagram in an easy to follow yet comprehensive way, showing how you can implement Instagram into your marketing strategy.

The Instagram platform was created as a photo-sharing social network; so, where does business fit in? While the platform may have started as a social network for sharing photos, it has morphed into an excellent way to kick-start a business, reach sales goals, and connect with consumers. There are currently over 1-billion active monthly users on Instagram. Why not get your piece of the 1-billion customer pie?

In the following chapters, you will discover how to market effectively on Instagram. This includes everything from creating a profile, to choosing hashtags, to running paid advertising. No matter your goals for marketing on Instagram, the information in this book will be able to help you achieve them.

Thank you again for taking the time to read this book. I hope you find it to be both interesting and informative. Let's begin!

Chapter 1: Growing Your Business With Instagram

It is no surprise that Instagram has grown to be a powerful and influential social media platform. It accounts for upwards of 55.8 percent of the total social network users in the United States. Instagram's greatest popularity lies with millennials and teen demographics. Yet, this is not just simply an American social network. Actually, upwards of 80 percent of users are international. It is quite clear that Instagram presents many different opportunities for businesses to capitalize on. One of the greatest misconceptions that businesses have is that the picture-centric nature of Instagram makes it a bad fit for their brand.

The key here is to find the ways that Instagram can work for your business. You need to understand how to develop content that helps highlight your brand.

Setting up your business account

The first thing you are going to do after you have created your account is to write a short bio. Within your bio, you need to identify to your followers what you are about in a succinct and catchy fashion.

Think of it as summarizing your brand in a way that reflects how you want others to see you. The formula we suggest you use is following

1. Brand philosophy
2. Brand hashtag
3. Social Network handle
4. Website Link

So just for example let's say my company is a Taco Truck. In that case, my bio might look something like this:

Taco Tuesday Truck
Live like every day is Taco Tuesday!
#TacoTuesdayEveryDay
@TacoTuesdayEveryDay
www.TacoTuesdayTruck.com

Also, remember if you have a brick and mortar location, or perhaps multiple locations, include that information as well. This could simply be putting in the address of your phsycial location.

One of the most important things for brands to do is include a link back to their site within their bio. Instagram wants to keep people on its platform, which is why adding links into comments will not work. You cannot include hyperlinks in posts or comments on the platform. The only place you are allotted to post a link is within the bio. This also means that you should link your most important link in your bio. Often this will link back to a brand's main page, newest products, or most recent blog post.

Your username is another important aspect of your social presence. Not just on Instagram, but across all social platforms. It's a great idea to make sure that you can grab the name you want on all popular platforms, even if you do not currently plan to market in these locations.

Ideally, you would want that user name to match your business name. Unfortunately, that will not always be possible. So you should find something that is as close as possible. You can consider using abbreviations, variations, or underscores, but ultimately you want to match your brand name as closely as possible.

The next part that is important when setting up your account is your photo. You have many options when you choose a photo for your page. You can use your logo, a product, storefront, or even a shot of your employees at work. The type of photo is not as important as the message you wish to inspire with your brand.

Creating Posts

Instagram is a visual social network; with that said, brands and influencers should focus on top-quality visuals. So to make your Instagram engaging and successful, you need to stand out visually. This is not to say that your products need to be beautiful on their own, although it would be helpful if they are, but that your brand should have a cohesive, well-lit, and high-quality imagery.

Here are some basic rules for Insta-Visuals:

1. Lighter images are more successful – typically these images receive 24% more likes than darker ones.

2. Greater background space and less busy – typically these images receive 29% more likes.

3. Color branding – Focus on one color of your brand and allow it to dominate. Images that have a dominating tone or color get 17% more likes.

Editing tools are an excellent way to make your photos more appealing. If you haven't yet, it would be wise to consider your brand's color scheme. This can help you to determine the overall feel of your Instagram feed.

You may choose to use muted pastels, desaturated neutrals, or vivid brights. The point here is to find a style that is suitable for your brand. You can then use editing tools to help your images work cohesively together.

For example, referring back to our Taco Truck, we might focus on vivid colors against black or white backdrops. The wonderful thing is that Instagram has built-in filters that are a great place to start when developing the look of your feed. As you move into more of a manual approach, you may consider downloading the Adobe Lightroom App, which gives you even more creative editing freedom over your images.

One clear thing that you should remember is people do not want to be sold to. A rule of thumb to use on all social networks is the 80/20 rule of selling. Ideally, you want to use Instagram to drive traffic back to your website or to your physical location. However, when you get too pushy with your sales pitch, you are actually working counterintuitively to your goal.

The 80/20 rule suggests that you focus 80 percent of your content on engaging followers and not your pushing your products or services. That leaves the other 20% of your posts to be used for encouraging followers to make a purchase. This might sound counterintuitive, but people go to Instagram for entertainment, not to be bombarded with advertisements.

Refrain from using the old-school, flyer type advertisements. These are turn-offs for your Instagram followers. Rather, take a more subtle approach in how you are sharing your products or services. A brand that is really great at this process is Pinky Up Tea @pinkyuptea – They use a great mix of advertising and subliminal marketing to create a cohesive brand image on Instagram.

One of the greatest ways to succeed on Instagram is to focus on "lifestyle" content rather than simply the products alone. This is where some additional research may be necessary for your brand. You need to determine the lifestyle content that will be most engaging for your followers. You can do this in many ways through market research within your customer base.

Here are some questions to ask yourself when thinking about the lifestyle of your followers.

1. Who is your ideal customer?
2. What hobbies, dreams, and interests does this person have?
3. Where do they eat, drink, shop, and play?
4. What music do they like?

5. Do they read books? Watch TV?

Go back to our Taco Truck example from before. You could assume that their customers are individuals who are on the move, love Mexican food, have busy days, and are out late at night. Now, think about the type of content that may appeal to these individuals. Take a moment and brainstorm some ideas that may resonate with your audience.

Another thing that fans love is when you take their images and feature them. You may have noticed that some of your favorite Instagram feeds are not pictures from the company or brand, but ones repurposed from fans. One way that brands are gathering this content is through specific brand hashtags or suggesting that fans tag your business. This lets you see what your customers are saying, and then you can turn around and feature this content on your feed as well. This is an exceptional way to source great content and create brand loyalty at the same time! Your followers feel special and appreciated, and your feed becomes more authentic. It also provides social proof to potential future customers that your products and services are high quality.

Another powerful way to share content on Instagram is through the use of Stories. Stories are a video feature that was created to be in direct competition with the Snapchat app's story feature. This is a great way for your brand to make personal connections with the audience. With stories, you can show followers behind the scenes photos and footage of things that happen within your business. Some brands are using their stores to provide sneak peeks into upcoming launches as well. Your followers want to know what's happening, and when you let them behind the scenes, they feel more engaged.

Hashtags are necessary

Okay, so that old saying that less is more completely does not apply to Instagram. When it comes to hashtags and Instagram, it's time to go all out. Research shows that using more than five hashtags increases the amount of engagement and interactions with a post. Furthermore, the posts with greater than eleven hashtags have the greatest interactions. It is important to remember that Instagram does limit you to a maximum of 30 hashtags per post or comment. My suggestion is to keep your hashtags to between 15-20. This way, you do not seem too spammy, and you get the maximum exposure.

To locate the best hashtags for your brand, you will need to do a bit of research. There are many tools available on the internet like RiteTag, or Hashtagify, which can help you find popular hashtags. You will want to spend some time coming up with a set of hashtags that are relevant to your customers and your brand.

The placement of your hashtags is also important. You don't always want to place them in the text of your post, but instead, in the first comment under your post. This is with the exception of brand-specific hashtags. By placing the hashtags in the comments, you are visually separating the hashtags from the post, giving your post a cleaner look.

You may also want to create your own branded hashtags; these are a great way to bring authenticity to your brand. They also encourage engagement with your brand. The process for doing this is very simple. You may like to create a hashtag out of your brand name, or alternatively, create a hashtag that is totally unique. Going back to our Taco Truck example, we may choose to use #TacoTuesdayEveryDay as our branded hashtag. Think for a moment, what could your brand's hashtag be?

Perks for your followers

Take your Instagram beyond simple content creation and subliminal lifestyle promotion; your Instagram is also an excellent place to share discounts, sales, and promotions. The best way to do this is to mention sales or promotions in the captions of your photos, or even through overlays on your images. Online design tools like Canva allow you to create text overlays for your graphics where you can advertise a promotion. One key thing to remember is links are only available in your bio, so you may need to update your bio link to point to the promotion.

Contests are another amazing way to drive engagement on Instagram. Instagram is perfect for hosting contests; by creating a specific hashtag for that contest, you can encourage fans of your brand to participate by taking their own photos and using your hashtag for a chance to win whatever you deem the prize to be. This also gives you a great supply of content to use in the future!

Not only are your followers entering a contest, but they are also doing promotional work for you. When they mention your brand in their images, your business then gets exposed to a whole different audience. This allows you to connect with demographics that you previously may not have targeted.

Tracking Efficiency

Honestly, all of the things above will not matter much if you are not doing something to track your efforts. As you develop your Instagram strategy, you need to keep in mind what your goals are for building your presence on the platform.

Typically, this means finding key metrics to track and monitor. Depending on your goal, you want to see your efforts moving your brand closer to that goal. So, if your goal is to increase your presence on Instagram overall, you may focus on growing your followers or increasing likes on posts. Alternatively, you may be more focused on the sales aspect of your brand and increasing conversion rates. In this instance, you would want to measure clicks to your site and your sales performance.

Tracking tools are a great way to measure your success once you have identified what success looks like to you. Instagram offers access to key metrics that you will want to pay close attention to. The insights report provides metrics for impressions, reach, engagement, and top posts.

As well, you can have the ability to review your demographics so you can find out the makeup of your audience from age, sex, and even where the majority are located. Knowing who you are reaching can help you to adjust your content to increase follow, likes, and become more engaging for your audience.

Chapter 2: Instagram Influencer Status

Influencers are making a huge splash on all social networks, but Instagram might be the platform where they are most prominent. Insta influencers are a hugely successful portion of the users on Instagram. However, achieving that influencer status is not easy.

One thing to remember when trying to become an influencer is that growth is an uphill battle, and it will take some time. One of the best things to know is that to be an influencer you do not have to have hundreds of thousands of followers. Micro-influencers can be very powerful in some industries. Regardless of where you are currently on your Instagram journey, there are a few strategies that can help you on the way to influencer status.

As an influencer, you want to begin by identifying content pillars and finding your specific niche. Companies that market through Instagram influencers are looking for images that resonate with their brand. Focus on becoming an influencer in a specific industry or field by posting content that will resonate with the brands and businesses in that niche.

How do you find your niche?

- What is my passion?

- What am I already knowledgeable about?
- What type of content could I consistently provide?

Once you have identified your niche, you can then move onto your content pillars. The process of using content pillars helps make it easier for you to rotate your content between each day. A content pillar is more a more specific topic that guides the content you post.

So, think back to our Taco Truck. The pillars of content could be: Mexican Food, Street Style, Fresh Ingredients.

So, the weeks' content calendar might look something like this:

- Monday: Mexican Food (Taco)
- Tuesday: Street Life (Picture of the Truck on the street)
- Wednesday: Fresh Ingredients (Close up of Limes)
- Thursday: Mexican Food (Picture of Nachos)
- Friday: Street Life (Picture of To-Go cup on the counter)
- Saturday: Mexican Food (Person eating Taco)
- Sunday: Fresh Ingredients (Close up of Jalapenos)

It is a great idea to use a service like *Planoly* or *Later* to plan out your content. This way, you can focus on running your business and engaging with your fans rather than constantly creating content. Visual planners also allow you to see what your feed will look like, and make sure that you are keeping a cohesive look to your feed.

Consistency

At the beginning of Instagram, it was possible to post only sporadically and still grow consistently. However, over time the platform has changed greatly. If you want to see growth on Instagram, you have to stay in your follower's minds. This makes it vital that you are consistent with your content.

When thinking of your feed, determine a schedule for how often you will post. You might choose to post seven days a week, or perhaps just Monday through Friday. If you do choose to only post to your feed Monday through Friday, it is recommended to post on your Instagram Stories every single day. Stories have become increasingly more engaging than actual feed posts. More and more people are spending an increased amount of time viewing stories rather than scrolling through Instagram feeds.

Understandably, it is hard to stay consistent and show up every day. One solution is to batch your content. Dedicate time to shoot the next week's content; this could mean teaming up with a photographer and shooting lots of different shots to give you enough variety in content to last you for a few weeks. Always refer back to your content pillars to make sure you are maintaining alignment with your brand.

Captions

The days of simple captions are long gone. Influencers today are creating almost a microblog with each Instagram post on their feed. Users are wanting more from their influencers, and a pretty photo with a four-word caption just won't cut it. Since 2016, captions have jumped from simple 120-word descriptions to upwards of 400+ words, which is why we consider what you are putting in your caption closer to a microblog than a caption. There is great power in the caption; it is an opportunity to spark conversation and help create a community on your page. This is also where you, as a brand, are able to provide value to your audience.

So, as you are writing your captions, think more as though you are actually writing a blog post. Do remember however, that the caption should obviously relate to the image you have posted.

Now there are a few notable things to keep in mind when you are creating your captions. When scrolling Instagram, you only have a very small amount of space to grab the reader's attention without them having to press the 'more' button. This means that you need to be sure that the first line in your caption is powerful enough to stop them scrolling and convince them to keep on reading. Think of the first sentence you write as the headline.

Just like any good newspaper article, you need something that is going to draw their attention. An example of a good headline might be:

- Five things you need to hear...
- The guide you have been seeking...
- The truth about...
- Anyone ever feel like...
- The #1 Best...
- Do you know how to...
- Ever wonder...

The next important thing is to end your caption with a call-to-action. This is where you are going to ask your audience to comment by asking a question, or asking for their opinion.

Also, make sure you break up your caption – a one really long paragraph is too hard to read. You will lose your readers very quickly, so break up the paragraphs. Another good addition to your posts are emojis, as these help to further break up large blocks of text.

Building a Community

Growing your following and increasing your engagement rate are both important metrics for influencers. However, you should also pay attention to the community that you are cultivating on your page. It is not always a great thing to have a large audience if they do not trust or value your content. You want to ensure that your community has strong relationships within it. Building relationships is one of the most important factors for influencers regardless of the stage of their growth.

So how do you build a community? Start by having conversations after you post by sticking around for at least 30 minutes to engage with comments.

When you receive direct messages, it is imperative that you respond and have genuine conversations with people. You don't have to reply to every single person, especially if they are being rude, but openly and directly communicating with your followers helps to turn them in to lifelong fans.

The other key to building a community is to get your audience talking to each other. You can do this by asking the audience to engage with each other in the comments of a post.

Know Your Audience

The more you know about your audience's demographics, the more you are able to engage with the things they are interested in. To really succeed as a brand influencer, you need to know the people following you well. This will provide you with all the knowledge you need to ensure your content resonates with them.

This can also help you to ensure that when you are collaborating with other brands, that these are brands your audience and followers have an interest in. Another way to get to know your audience is to start up conversations in the comments. You can do things like ask your followers to tell you their opinion about something specific, or simply ask for feedback.

Using polls in your Instagram stories is another fun way to get your community interacting and participating. You can ask questions that are specific to your niche.

The content that you post needs to match that which your brand is wanting to interact with. If you are a travel agent, for example, and want to focus on luxury travel, then you would look to collaborate with luxury resorts by posting content that resonates with that niche.

Networking

Being consistent with your posts will only get you so far in your quest to grow your following. You will still have to put yourself out there to connect with other influencers and brands. But how exactly do you land collaborations with other brands?

One method is to use Instagram to influence marketing platforms like *Collectively*, *Fohr*, and *Popular Pays*. When you set up a profile, you can then be contacted by brands on the platform if feel you are a good fit for any of their campaigns.

You can also seek out public relations firms and introduce yourself via email. The key here is to not suggest any specific brand, but instead to simply ask them to keep you on their radar for any opportunities that might be a good fit in the future. If one of these organizations happen to be local to you, it's a great idea to organize a meetup in person.

It is also a great idea to create and send out a media kit. As you are pitching yourself to a new brand, make sure you have a media kit prepared. The next logical question is, what do I include in a media kit? Within your kit, you will include your social handles, website, audience size on each platform, following demographics, as well as examples of products that you may have used in your branding or other collaborations that you have done in the past.

Diversify

One thing to remember is that successful influencers do not solely rely on Instagram. Remember that you are only using Instagram's platform; you are a third party and have no control over the algorithm. When you grow your audience on other platforms, you increase your revenue potential and can connect with other brand collaborators.

Think of it like this - if you have a website with a blog and a brand approaches you to collaborate, instead of only posting to Instagram, you could also add a blog post, or send a promotional email to your fans and increase the reach significantly.

If you find being in front of the camera is easy for you, then YouTube might be the perfect spot for you to target after Instagram. If you are well-spoken, then you may find a podcast a better platform. If you love writing, then a blog may be just the thing you are looking for to increase your reach.

One of the best ways to increase your connection is by building your email list. This is incredibly important because these connections are ones that you "own," and you are not relying on any specific platform for that list to exist. Keep the following in mind when trying to build a quality email list:

- Think about the value you can provide your audience. What type of things are they struggling with? Maybe you send out a tutorial video or a PDF guide in exchange for them signing up to your email list.

- Creating a Freebie helps to grow your list – the freebie does not have to cost you an arm and a leg; it can be as simple as a PDF, and instructional video, or a template.

- Opt-in pages are a great way to grab potential customer email addresses as they snag your freebie in exchange for their email address. While there is a bit of technical knowledge needed here, you can use services such as AWeber, LeadPages, and MailChimp to simplify the process.

- Use your social channels to promote your list. To do this, simply post on Instagram, Facebook, and any other platforms you have a following on, and talk about the freebie you're giving away in exchange for them signing up to your list.

Chapter 3: Advertising on Instagram

Creating successful ads on Instagram is not overly hard. Users are already primed to shop on the platform, and with the increase in shoppable posts, there is more potential for sales.

So, what are Instagram ads? These are posts or stories that a brand or business pays to have shown to a wider audience. Often these posts will look very similar to regular feed posts but can be identified by a 'sponsored' label next to the post itself. These posts also include some type of call-to-action button.

The next big question when thinking about advertising on Instagram is the cost. There is no single figure that you can put on what the cost of an ad will be. However, as an advertiser, you have the flexibility to set your own desired budget from $5 to $50,000. You are in control, and can set your campaign spending limit.

There are many types of ads that you can run on Instagram, including photos, stories, videos, carousel, collection, IGTV, and Instagram Shopping ads. Every type of ad works a little differently and will suit different business goals; many even have different call-to-action options available.

Regardless of the ad type, the objective is to find a call-to-action that supports your goal. So before selecting an ad type, you should consider what your goal is. Do you wish to increase visitors to your website or profile? Do you want to encourage people to direct message you so you can create meaningful conversations? If a video ad is what you think will be most fitting for your brand, remember that you only have one minute to convince users to take action. Shorter videos are highly effective and require you to be very succinct in your message. Carousel ads offer the user a more interactive option as they allow the user to swipe through a series of images or videos with a call-to-action button pointing directly to your website. Collection ads on Instagram are great for e-commerce. These ads allow users to make purchases directly from the ad by taking the user to an Instant Experience Storefront. These ads are very powerful as they combine photos, videos, and direct-responses marketing in the one place.

Choosing the Best Ad Type

When you are ready to select an ad type, it is important to be sure that you are intentional with your selection of the ad format. Start by considering what your goal is with the ad, and also be sure to review your marketing strategy. Consider what type of ad will resonate best with your intended audience.

Creating an Ad on Instagram

There are two different ways that you can create ads for Instagram. The first is the easiest way, and that is directly through the app itself. This method offers a fair amount of customization and options to create a stunning Instagram, and the second way is by using Facebook Ads Manager.

Creating an ad within the app

The first and easiest way to begin is simply by promoting existing posts on your profile. If you are familiar with boosting posts on Facebook, this is very similar. It's ideal to select a post that is already performing well; this is a great method for reaching more users.

One thing to note is that you need to have a professional account to be able to create ads on Instagram. In your Instagram settings you simply need to select *'Switch to Professional Account'* to set this up. Once you have a professional account set up with your payment information, you can create ads from within Instagram itself.

If you have a Facebook account that is linked to your Instagram page, you can run ads from the Facebook ads manager, also.

Using the Facebook Ads Manager is a little bit different and allows you to take advantage of integrated performance. This means that you can run ads not only on Instagram but also on Facebook simultaneously. With Facebook Ads Manager, you can customize the audience and many other features while accessing the ability to monitor your ad's performance. If you haven't created a Facebook Profile, you will have to do this first.

Once you are logged into your Facebook account, you will need to choose the objective for your ad. You will begin by going to Ads manager and clicking '*Create*'.

Next, you will find that there are two different workflows you can choose from to create your Instagram ad. The service has a guided creation process, which will walk you through every step in creating a typical ad. This is a great choice if you are new to marketing. The second option, quick creation, gives you significant control over crafting your ad. Those with greater experience in creating ads often prefer to use this workflow.

For the process of this book, let's focus on the guided creation of the ad. We begin by selecting an objective from the ads manager's offer list. Each of these objectives are explained below:

- Brand Awareness – increases the awareness of your products or business among users who have yet to hear from you.

- Reach – This method shows ads to as many people as possible within your targeted demographic

- Traffic – This focuses on clicks for your website or any URL of your choice

- Engagement – This is derived from increasing the likes, comments, and shares to a post

- Video – This shows your videos to those that might be most interested in viewing it

- Lead Generation – Allows you to gather lead data from the   ad

- Messages – Focuses on getting customers to connect directly with your brand's account.

After you identify the objective of your ad, you will be prompted to name the campaign. The default name will just be the objective you selected; however, you can choose to select a more specific name to keep track of the different campaigns you are running. It would be wise to create easily identifiable names for your ad campaigns, as over time you may end up running multiple campaigns at once.

The next task you will have to complete is identifying the audience you are targeting. The good thing is that Facebook owns Instagram, so you have access to a large selection of targeting options. These options go beyond standard demographics and allow you to craft a message that is unique and applies you your specific niche.

After you have selected your demographics, you are now ready to select the placement. You have a few different options when it comes to placement, and you can choose to place your ad automatically or manually. When you place your ad automatically, it will be shown to the audience where it is most likely to perform best. When you choose manual placement, you have the option to manually pick and choose the locations the ad appears. You may choose to limit your ad to only appearing on Instagram Stories or only Instagram Feeds.

After you have made all the above choices, you can then set your budget and schedule. As you choose your daily budget, you get to decide the maximum amount you want to spend both daily, and over the lifetime of the ad campaign.

Finally, choose your ad and prepare the content and formatting that will resonate with your niche. Finishing up is pretty simple from here on out. You simply choose your pictures or video you'd like to advertise, the text accompanying your ad, and then click confirm. That's all there is to it. You have created your first Instagram ad!

Chapter 4: Marketing Strategies

Marketing strategies have been around for quite some time, and many of the same techniques you may have previously used in your business can also be applicable to Instagram marketing.

When you think marketing strategy, it is really quite simply your game plan for how you will approach a specific product or aspect of your business. For the purposes of this book, we are looking at your strategy for Instagram, with your goal being to attract customers through promoting your products.

It's time to think of your brand's big picture vision and how your marketing plan can address it to tackle goals and bring a strategy to life. This chapter is focused on helping you devise a strategy for your Instagram marketing efforts.

SWOT Analysis

The best thing to do when starting out is to run a SWOT Analysis. This will help you to identify what your strengths, weaknesses, opportunities, and threats are in the marketplace. This is a vital step in the planning process and is a great opportunity to gather perspectives from other members of your organization. When you include others from your organization, you are able to look at things with less of a bias and gain different perspectives. When possible, get as many fellow colleagues to contribute as you can. When you have a clear perspective of the things you are excelling at, where you need improvement, and are aware of both the risks and potential opportunities, you will be able to design an effective marketing strategy much more easily.

What Is SWOT?

Business is full of acronyms, and SWOT is just one of the many you will come across. You may already be aware that SWOT stats for –strengths, weaknesses, opportunities, and threats. Understanding where your business fits within each of these areas can provide great insight into your brand's marketing strategy.

Using a SWOT analysis when creating your Instagram page helps you to focus your marketing plan in a way that traditionally, many brands do not. This process forces you to evaluate your business and determine your strengths and weaknesses within the industry, as well as the potential opportunities or threats you may face. Pinpointing some of these areas can be difficult, and it may require you to be brutally honest with yourself about your brand and its place within the industry.

Creating the SWOT Framework

Developing your brand's SWOT framework starts by creating a two-by-two gird. You will label each cell with S, W, O, T to represent strengths, weaknesses, opportunities, and threats. It will look something like this:

Strengths	Weaknesses
Opportunities	Threats

Looking at the first quadrant of the table, strengths are internally what your brand does well. If you were to describe your brand with just a few keywords, what would they be? Ask yourself the following questions:

- What are the things that your brand does well?

- What makes your brand unique?

- What sets you apart?

The goal here is to gain a clear understanding of what your brand's unique strengths are.

The next step is hard for many brands, and that is to admit their weaknesses.. This is where you need to be completely honest with yourself. Where is your business lacking?

Is your brand name too long or too hard to remember? Identifying that people cannot remember your brand name as an issue is a common weakness among brands. Possibly your weakness is inventory levels, which can make it hard to promote some products because you are struggling with in-stock issues. The goal here is to identify a few key areas that you can improve.

The next quadrant requires you to analyze potential opportunities. When you are looking to determine what opportunities may be available to you, look for where the gaps are occurring in the market. Let's go back to the example of our Taco Truck from before. Most food trucks are focused only on the lunch rush Monday – Friday. The Taco Truck may find that hitting the Friday and Saturday night bar scene as a great opportunity to grow their business. The business may find that some of the young professionals that are heading out on Friday and Saturday night turn into loyal customers for their lunch Monday – Friday.

Opportunities occur where gaps exist. So, think for a moment, what gaps exist for your brand?

What is something your brand could do that others are not?

What new service could you offer to solve a pain point for potential customers?

The last quadrant is one that many people really dislike identifying. This is the threats they face. This is typically where brands put themselves on the defensive. Yet, it is exceptionally important to know what could hurt your brand. Especially if your brand is small or just starting out, you may find that there are bigger brands that can undercut your prices because of the scale they are able to produce at. You may also face threats from regulations. This is where you have to admit and consider where you are vulnerable. The task here is simply to identify where your brand is most vulnerable. Being aware of these vulnerabilities will allow you to put strategies in place to mitigate these threats as much as possible.

Improving your SWOT analysis - What you may not know

Okay, so you have developed your brand's SWOT grid, and now you want to know how you compare to the rest of your industry. It is important to understand that all brands have strengths, weaknesses, opportunities, and threats that they may not be aware of. This is where the comments and posts play a role in uncovering additional information—listening as a brand is just as important as engaging. Sometimes it can even be more important, and this just happens to be one of those times.

Where to look for strengths – Embrace the hearts

Your community will tell you what they like about your brand. When they mention you or use your brand hashtags, this is them showing you love. Through this, you are able to qualitatively analyze what they specifically are loving from your brand.
In the comments, what keywords are followers using to describe you?

Where to look for weaknesses – Read ALL the comments

You may already have a following large enough to find out what fans are not liking about your product. This is even more important than finding out what people love about your brand. This is where you need to tune in without getting defensive.

Pay attention to any and all negative comments. More and more consumers are giving specific reasons as to why they hate something about a brand. These reasons can be anything from shipping times, website access, or the images you use.

The point here is to learn what the community sees as your weakness or areas for improvement. Sometimes it can be hard to identify or admit your weaknesses on your own, so pay close attention to what your customers say!

How to find the opportunities – filling in the blanks
When you are looking for opportunities, your social listening skills need to be on point. You need to understand what your target audience or niche is asking for.

To do this, you might do a bit of research and find out how a potential customer may be feeling in general about the product or service your brand represents. With this, you could simply take to Instagram and research your service. See what users of the platform are saying about services similar to what you offer. This can allow you to find out what the gap is between what the users are looking for and what you are currently offering. See what common complaints your competitors receive, and from there, figure out how you can provide a superior product or service that addresses those complaints.

This is where you are looking to solve some type of pain-point your target niche has, or to enhance their experience.

Using the Data to Formulate a Strategy

Now you have all the data gathered and are ready to formulate a plan for your Instagram strategy. Begin with putting your strengths front and center. These are the things that you know you are good at and can excel at. You might even like to mention these strengths in your Instagram bio.

The next step is to make sure your marketing plan focuses on communicating those strengths. As a brand, you have the option to focus directly on your strengths, or to take a more subtle approach.

Once again, let's use the example of our Taco Truck. One of the strengths they might have is the farm to table aspect; let's assume that they are the only food truck that procures all their produce and meats from local growers. This sets them apart as being a farm to table option with super fresh ingredients. Being farm to table is a strength for this brand, so they plan to publish a post each day that teaches consumers about the benefits of supporting local growers. They also plan to post once per week about how fresh ingredients makes a big difference in their quality.

The best way to do this is to create a content calendar for posting. This will help you map out what content to post when and allow you to focus in on your strengths throughout the month. The Taco Trucks calendar may look something like this:

S u	Mo	Tu	We	Th	Fr	Sa
	Post about Fresh Ingredients	Taco Tuesday Deal	Educational Post about Farm to Table	Post about Fresh Ingredients	Post about Weekend Events	Post about Fresh Ingredients

As you find more and more strengths for your brand, you will be able to sprinkle them into your content calendar. Ultimately you want to build a strong content calendar on the front end, so when you are heading out to shoot photos for your brand, you have a guideline as to what you need to capture on the front side. This way, you are not always chasing content. Your content should very much be a planned process.

While, in some instances, ignorance may be bliss, it could end up being the death of your social media presence or even brand. Not being able to admit or see your weaknesses is dangerous for any brand. It would be best if you prepared yourself to listen and take criticism from your followers and customers.

It is important to remember to include time for social listening within your strategy for Instagram. The best way to do this is to have your brand follow some specific hashtags to monitor your business. It is important to set time aside to review any mentions and respond to direct messages. There are lots of different social media management tools that you can use to help you with monitoring your brand. We will get to those later on in the book.

When you receive positive reviews, these are great content to repost in your story or use throughout your feed. Understand that while the hope is that everything will be rainbows and butterflies, it is quite possible that you will receive negative feedback or reviews also. When this happens, before you go on the defensive, look for specific evidence that you are not fulfilling the needs of your customer.

Consider the following:

- What was the consumer's expectation?
- Was there a miscommunication in the product description?
- Were the instructions confusing?

One best practice is to keep a log of what you uncover from feedback, especially the feedback that is negative. It could be as simple as a spreadsheet formatted like this:

What did customers comment	Post Link	Customer needs

You can also use this same method to identifies gaps within your industry.

Utilizing Opportunities

Once you have identified gaps within your industry, it is important to begin then to experiment with ways that you can provide services or products to fill these gaps. This, on the brands part, requires the willingness to take risks and try things that you may not have seen anyone else do before.

This is the point where you need to trust your research and take the leap. This could involve a variety of things, from partnering with an influencer to working with another brand.

Let's say you are a fashion brand, and you often get questions about items to accessorize your clothes with. This may be where you could find an accessory brand to partner with. You could then promote each other's products and mutually benefit.

Collaboration is an amazing tool to boost your brand into markets that it may not previously have been targeting before.

Reach out to reduce threats

It is highly likely that you are not the only brand in your industry. The big question is how do you reduce the threats to your brand? Many threats arise when you stop paying attention to the day-to-day actions of your brand and get lazy with reviewing your SWOT analysis. The best way to combat this is to take an active approach of listening and looking around. This will help you to identify threats as they are approaching, not as a reaction to something that has already occurred. One pro tip that many social media marketing professionals use is to keep a list of their competitors. They then regularly look to see what their competition is doing, and what kind of promotions they are running.

Actionable Strategy

The next part of your SWOT framework is to apply everything you have learned and create an actionable strategy. As you implement your plan, it is important to have a clear direction you'd like to go. With the data you have collected, you will be primed to build a list of actionable ideas, and design ways to make them happen operationally within your brand.

As a brand, you should consider

- What support will each tactic need?
- With what frequency will these tactics need to be evaluated?
- What does success look like for my brand?

Using a SWOT analysis can give you a never-ending amount of information to help you be actionable in your strategy. It is an exceptional way for those just starting out in business to see what is currently working in the market, where gaps exist, and what threats could be hazardous to their brand. When you pay close attention to the information a SWOT analysis provides and design your marketing strategy based upon this information, you will find yourself with a winning strategy for Instagram.

Assessing Your Value Proposition

You cannot have a strong marketing strategy without knowing your brand's value proposition. The value proposition should be focus on the strengths identified in the SWOT analysis. It should also be unique to your business. What value can you provide that your competition cannot, or does not currently? It is imperative that you identify this unique value proposition and focus on it relentlessly in your marketing efforts.

Identify the Objectives for Your Marketing Strategy

Just as your brand identifies its goals and objectives, you should do the same with your social media goals and objectives. Just as with any objective for your brand, you want to make sure that your objectives are measurable and time bound. When you do this, you are able to measure the success of your efforts against specific targets. A good place to start when developing your Instagram plan is to focus on three to five specific objectives. Then, re-evaluate these objectives quarterly or semi-annually depending on the time frame that is most suitable for your brand.

Chapter 5: Monetizing Your Instagram

Of course, as a brand, you want to monetize your Instagram account. However, remember to play the long game, and focus on giving value first before trying to ask your followers to buy anything from you.

Before monetizing, you have to build a following, and that means cultivating relationships with your followers and your brand. You have to show them the service that you provide and what's in it for them.

It all begins with creating a following; you need to grow your brand's account before you attempt to sell. You need to provide practical solutions and engage with your followers. This is to say, you need to engage with those who have similar interests to your brand - the only way to win on Instagram or any other social media platform is to be social.

Connect

So, where do you begin? One of the best techniques is to carefully select a few hashtags to engage with. These should relate to your brand. Take a moment and think about the ten most relevant hashtags that relate you your brand or industry. You can use a site like berst-hastags.com to help you identify the top hashtags for your brand.

If we are using out Food Truck Example from before, we might identify these as the top hashtags for our Food Truck:

#foodtruck
#food
#foodporn
#foodie
#streetfood
#foodtrucks
#foodphotorgapy
#foodstagram
#foodlover

Or these for Farm to Table:

#farmtotable
#eatlocal
#organic
#farmtofork
#food
#foodie
#supportlocal
#farmlife
#farmfresh

The great thing about searching hashtags is it becomes quite easy to identify tags that will fit with your niche. For example, once we have searched '#farmtotable', Instagram automatically will start recommending similar tags to follow. While the most popular hashtags may have millions of views, it is much harder to make an impact with these. It is better to find hashtags that relate to your brand but are lesser-known. This way, you will have less competition and can get yourself in front of an audience that is very specific to your brand.

Once you have identified your top hashtags, the next step is to spend a few moments scrolling through the top 10 posts for each hashtag. As you find a post that resonates with you, check the person's bio out. Look at what they like, their activity, what they dislike. Then you are ready to go back, read the content, and engage in the post. By taking this time to click the bio, you are arming yourself with information that can help you better engage with the individual.

One of the key things here is to pay attention to the engagement for that account. They may only have a few hundred followers, but each post they make might generate significant likes and comments. This could be a sign that this person is an influencer that you should reach out to and connect with. Micro-influencers like this can be extremely valuable to work with, particularly when you are first starting out.

Through this process, you are going to review your selected hashtags and find posts that you can comment on. This allows you to provide value outside of your brand. When you comment on others' posts, you can share the thoughts you have about the post. If you admire the content or aesthetic, this is a great place to say so. If you see someone ask a question and you can provide the answer, do so. The point here is to grow through posting and replying.

If you see that the content reminds you of another account, tag them if you know that they will benefit from seeing the post. You don't need to spend an inordinate amount of time doing this. Your goal is simple interaction and authenticity, and a little goes a long way if you're doing this regularly. As you continue to regularly do this, you will find that the connections become more and more meaningful, and you may even find your direct messages begin to increase.

It is really pretty easy; you just continue to do this and engage on Instagram every day. Remember, you should approach Instagram with the mentality to give more than you take. This process has been the strategy of successful social media professionals for years.

Identify

The next process is to identify every company in your industry, and determine who is doing it best, and who is underperforming in their marketing efforts. If you are running a Taco Truck, you might search for *'food Truck'* and review the tags, and the pages posting them.

The next step can be scary for some and push you out of your comfort zone, but if you want to collaborate with other brands, you have to reach out to them. Reaching out can be as simple as getting them on the phone and finding out who from their organization is in charge of collaboration - or sending a direct message to the brand's social media page. The thing here is if you never reach out, you do not know what their response would be. The key here is to tell the organization what you can offer to them. Just like engaging with your community, collaborators want to know what is in it for them.

Once you have built a following that trusts you and enjoys your content, you can begin to monetize your page. You can do so through collaborations, or through offering a product or service for sale directly to your followers. However, remember to continue providing value and posting quality content. For long-term success on Instagram, always give more than you take.

Chapter 6: Understanding the Instagram Algorithm

When Instagram made the decision to go away from chronological feeds, so many questions were prompted by influencers and brands. If it isn't chronological, how do followers see the posts from their favorite brands? Is video ranked higher than photos? Are hashtags good or bad?

Instagram went on record in January 2020 and addressed some key rumors about its controversial algorithm. Specifically stating the following:

- Ranking is impacted by Likes, Comments, Shares, and Views

- Video and Photo Posts are Equal in importance to the algorithm

- The algorithm is constantly changing because of user trends

- The algorithm identifies fake accounts, and they are not taken into consideration

- Business, influencer, and User accounts are all equal

- The first 30 minutes of performance does not determine the ranking on Instagram

Looking a bit closer at each of these, we find that Instagram wanted to put these rumors to bed.

On Instagram, photos and video are treated equally. The algorithm has a zero bias tolerance when it comes to if the content is a video or a photo. However, the algorithm does prioritize the type of content that a user engages with most. So those users who are more engaged with video will be shown more video in their feed. This is important for brands to take note of. The format of a video is designed in a way for a longer viewing period, which means the user spends more time on that format. Video also takes up a larger portion of the Explore page on Instagram, so this can also be an advantage for brands.

Instagram's algorithm is a learning algorithm, and it is able to spot bots and their comments on posts quickly, which helps to remove these tactics from affecting the ranking of posts or brands on Instagram. The best way for any brand to build engagement is through authenticity and sharing on the platform.

Another aspect that was under question is if the comment length matters. According to Instagram, all comments are taken into account. This includes comments that are strictly emojis. Comments are just one way for Instagram to indicate engagement within the algorithm. So, it is always a good idea to ensure you have a process where you reply to all comments on your pots. Not only can this keep the conversation moving on your post, it can help you show up in the algorithm.

The next big myth is that the type of account you have matters. Regardless of if you have a personal, business, or creator account, all accounts are created equal. Many influencers initially were worried about switching their profile to a business account, though ultimately this has zero effect on how your posts will perform.

Newer posts are not simply pushed higher in the algorithm because they are new. Posts can still gain traction well past the 30-minute mark. However, it is a best practice to ensure you are sharing content when your audience is there to engage. Optimizing your posting is just a good social media practice regardless of the platform. It can be tricky to manage and find the sweet spot, but when you do, you will see just how beneficial it can be in improving the engagement with your fans.

Key Factors That Influence the Algorithm

Six factors influence the Instagram algorithm; interest, relationship, timeliness, frequency, following, and usage. The Instagram algorithm is a learning machine, so it is always changing and improving.

The first thing that the algorithm does is predicts how much a user cares about a post. User's feeds are not simply filled with just the people they follow; they are also filtering the content that the user likes. As the algorithm identifies posts that it believes the user will like, these types of posts will appear more frequently in the feed. The algorithm uses the user's past behaviors on content to analyze and determine what the user would most likely want to see. This means that the user's feed is simply a compilation of user behaviors on Instagram. It looks at the people the user interacts with frequently, which stories they watch, and the people tagged in photos, along with the type of posts that the user comments on and likes.

Engagements are important to the algorithm. Instagram values posts that are being commented on, reshared, liked, and viewed. The more engaging the content, the more people it will be shown to.

The algorithm also decides what your relationship is with your followers. Instagram's algorithm wants to prioritize posts from family, friends and accounts the user cares about. So, the more you interact with people, the more Instagram identifies these interactions and shows you their content. This is why, for brands, it is important to interact and engage with their audience so that the algorithm determines there is a relationship between the brand and the user.

So theoretically, Instagram decides who a user cares about based on the way they use the app. Here are some of the things that Instagram looks at when observing your behavior on the app:

- Users, you know in your real life
- Users and brands that you search for
- Those who you direct message
- The content you like

You may notice that when you first start following someone you that you see more and more of that person's content in your feed. However, if you fail to engage with their content, you are signaling to the algorithm that you are no longer as interested in that content anymore.

This is why it is important for brands to post consistently on Instagram. This can be either through posting in your stories or on your feed daily.

As a brand, consistently posting good content is not only going to improve your engagement, but it also signals the algorithm that you have a quality account. When it comes to a brand's posting frequency, this will greatly fall back onto what the brand can manage and its business goals. It is not a great idea to try a posting strategy that you cannot maintain. It is better to build a consistent schedule that you can maintain. So, if your brand is consistent and committed to posting daily, then do that. If they are only committed to posting a few times a week, then do that. The key here is to not flip flop. You need to be consistent. As well you should never compromise the quality of a post just for the sake of getting something posted.

Many bands use free schedulers to help them with their consistency in posting. These schedulers allow them to batch their work photos, captions, and even hashtags from the web. When you batch your work, this can save a significant amount of time, leaving you with extra time to focus on other areas of your Instagram strategy.

Services like Later and Planoly offer auto-publish features, without push notifications. This allows your posts to be posted during your day automatically.

Another pro tip is to treat comments like a conversation. You should never leave a comment without a response; as we have shared before, it is all about engagement and building relationships with your fans.

An increase in the number of direct messages you are receiving shows that you are engaging with your fans. Just like with comments, be sure that you are responding to all direct messages you receive.

Timeliness

The algorithm does not simply look at the engagement of a post on Instagram. It also takes into consideration the length of time from when the photo was posted. It appears that the algorithm is not only showing the most interesting posts to you, but is actually favoring the more recent ones. This is why it's important to find the best time for you to post on Instagram. If you are posting when your followers are online, you automatically increase your chances of those posts being seen and engaged with.

The best way to find out when your fans are the most active is to use Instagram insights. This allows you to see the specific times of day that your audience is most active. These times may vary during the week, so it is important to understand that weekend posts might need to be posted at different time slots than weekday posts. The best time to post will depend highly on where your followers are located, and the demographic that you are targeting.

Instagram also looks at the frequency of your posts. If you are a user that frequently scrolls, your feed will appear to be more chronological. This is because Instagram is showing you the best posts since you last visited. If you do not use the app very frequently, then Instagram will sort your content in a way that they think will be most interesting to you.

The algorithm also keeps an eye on who the user is following. It looks not only at who but how many people a user follows. If users have a lot of accounts they follow, it gives Instagram more options to choose content for the user. In these instances, it is much harder for a brand to be seen by that user. This is where you have to really focus on engagement. If that user has identified you as a brand that they comment on, and like frequently, it will push you up higher in their algorithm.

The Algorithm and Stories

The stories that a user sees first in their feed are stories that the user engages with most. These accounts are typically ones that the user has built a relationship with.

The stories algorithm puts a great amount of focus on timeliness, and wants to ensure that it is always showing the latest story from a user's favorite accounts. This is why you may find that many brands are posting more to their stories than to their feeds.

This is to help engage with users who are watching stories before scrolling.

Instagram's algorithm has identified that users want to see their favorite influencers and brands first, so they put them in the beginning spots.

To get featured sooner in stories, simply spend more time posting them; the more active you are in posting stories, the more likely Instagram is to jump you to the front of a person's queue. This is not to say that you have to be constantly in your phone posting stories or to your feed. Just like how you can batch your work with Later or Plannoly, you can also batch your stories too. This will help you to create content ahead of time, and then have it ready for direct posting when it is time.

Chapter 7: All About Hashtags

One of the most effective ways to get engagement and views on your content is through using hashtags. They are highly effective, and one of the key ways you can grow your opportunities for engagement. Posts with a minimum of one hashtag have an average of 12.6% greater engagement than posts without any hashtags at all. This is why your brand must have some kind of hashtag strategy as part of their marketing plan.

Since the beginning of Instagram, there have been many changes. However, one thing has remained constant, and that is the use and importance of hashtags on the platform. Brands who use targeted and relevant hashtags on their posts or stories will connect with more potential customers.

Think of hashtags like a directory if you will. Users who have public profiles and add a hashtag to their post will then be filtered into a hashtag page with all other videos or photos tagged with the same hashtag. The purpose of hashtags is to be able to discover content for users. As a brand, using the right hashtag at the right time can connect you with your target audience.

Once again, our Food Truck example might post a picture of some beautiful fresh produce and use the hashtags #organic #farmtofork #foodtrucksofig when they post the image. By using these hashtags, the image is then added to the catalog so users who follow those hashtags will see your post.

There are a few things brands should remember:

- Users with private profiles who tag posts will not show up on the hashtag page

- You can use numbers in your hashtag, however special characters and spaces are not allowed

- You can only tag your own content

- There is a limit of 30 hashtags on a post and ten hashtags on a story

Types of Hashtags

As a brand, it is important to understand that different types of hashtags fit with different audiences. The key here is to use the appropriate hashtags within your Instagram strategy.

Community

The first type of hashtag we will discuss are community hashtags. These are ones that connect a community of people together. A community on Instagram is typically made up of like-minded users around a specific subject. This is a perfect way to connect with your community and improve your searchability. Your community hashtags can be anything from a product or service like #tacotruck to the niche for your industry, such as #latenightfoodie.

Branded

This type of hashtag is one that is unique to your brand. It can be as simple as the brand tagline, company name, or product name. Or quite honestly, it could be a hashtag that has nothing to do with the brand name but resonates with the brand identity.

Unlike community hashtags that have the purpose of increasing the reach of your brand, branded hashtags are designed to connect your brand through different themes to your audience. They are also a great way for brands to gather user-generated content.

The goals you have with your branded hashtag is to get your followers to work for you. These hashtags encourage followers to share and talk about your brand. As they use your brand hashtag on their post, you will then be exposed to potential new audiences. Once you develop a branded hashtag, it is your job to remind customers to use it and share it in both their captions and their stories.

Campaign

Unlike community and branded hashtags that are meant to be long-lasting, campaign hashtags have a more short-term life. They may last a few days, a season, or even a year. Brands use short-term hashtags to tie specific campaigns to their social accounts. One example situation that a brand may use a branded hashtag is when they are launching a new product or hosting an event.

Finding the Best Hashtags

Using hashtags correctly on your Instagram account can be the difference between growth and stagnation of your brand. You want to be sure you are using a hashtag that will engage and attract followers.

Many hashtags are very popular and have been used millions of times over. However, this does not mean that you are going to get comments simply from adding those super-popular hashtags to your post. Rather than selecting the most popular hashtags from Instagram, it is more beneficial to your brand to use hashtags with fewer views that are more relevant to your market.

But where do you find these hashtags that are perfect for your community? Begin by first starting to look at your audience or niche and see what hashtags they are already using. There is nothing wrong with using a hashtag that is already trending within your market, so long as it makes sense with your post. Another method is to look at your competition and see what hashtags they are using, as well as the industry leaders. These are all great places to start to get inspiration for what hashtags may resonate with your brand.

A mistake that many brands make is simply throwing out random hashtags that mean nothing to their niche or brand. Make sure that you are doing your research and being tactical with the hashtags you use.

Chapter 8: Business Tools for Instagram

As the number of Instagram users continues to grow, businesses are working hard to find tools that can help them streamline their efforts. The following are some popular applications that can help your brand be successful on Instagram.

The first tool we suggest is LeeTags – this is a great tool for finding trending hashtags by just typing in a few keywords. It will also help you by analyzing the top and most relevant hashtags that you can use. Another key benefit of this app is that you can also save these hashtags into collections and subcategories so that you can micro-market.

Another recommended app is Pablo, which is a great tool to create designer graphics. Pablo allows brands to create content for their accounts and use images that bring in significant views and shares within the community. Another great thing about Pablo is it is an easy to use tool that allows you to upload your own images within the app. The fonts are beautiful, the graphics are on point, and you can create quotes that will fit perfectly with your brand.

Selling on Instagram can be really easy with apps like Shoppable. Enabling Shoppable Instagram posts allows you to open the e-commerce of your Instagram and seamlessly connect your followers with your services or products.

Lapse It is another great app that allows you to make amazing time-lapse videos with your mobile device. This can be really helpful when you are showing behind the scenes video in stories, such as showing yourself setting up for an event, or demonstrating how a product is made.

Magisto is another video app that brands can use to create videos in minutes. You simply submit your raw footage to the app, then choose the style and collection along with what music fits the video.

Horizon is an application that allows you to capture vertical videos and convert them into horizontal videos. Horizon is an app that is packed with other features like tilt and zoom, filters, slow motion, and lots more. If you plan to use video in your strategy, Horizon is an app that should be included on the shortlist to check out.

The last app that should also be on your shortlist, especially if you do not have a graphic designer on staff, is Canva. This service is available both as an app, and also as a web application that is loaded with many features that are simple and easy to use. It has an extensive library of content that is ready-to-publish yet highly customizable. It also has built in catalogs to help you stay on track with your brand fonts and colors. If you are just starting and there is no room in the budget for your own graphic designer, Canva is a must-have tool for creating amazing posts and engaging content quickly.

Conclusion

You should now feel equipped with a wide range of knowledge about Instagram and how to market your business or brand on the platform. As you put this platform to work for your brand, remember that authenticity is of top importance. Remember to provide value before you ask your followers to buy anything from you. Focus on building relationships with your followers, and over time you will gain a loyal following that will support you over the long run!

Remember to be patient in your Instagram strategy. Don't expect results overnight. Remain consistent, and within 6-12 months of following a solid content and marketing plan, you should be seeing great success!

I'd like to thank you for taking the time to read this book. I hope you have found it to be both interesting and informative, and I wish you the best of luck in your Instagram endeavors!

www.ingramcontent.com/pod-product-compliance
Lightning Source LLC
LaVergne TN
LVHW050149060326
832904LV00003B/72